The George Verdak Collection

Eras of the Dance

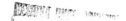

The George Verdak Collection

Eras of the Dance

Montgomery Museum of Fine Arts
Montgomery, Alabama
December 10, 1976 through January 13, 1977

Huntsville Museum of Art
Huntsville, Alabama
April 11, 1976 through May 22, 1976

Table of Contents

Acknowledgments

George Verdak is Director of the Indianapolis Ballet
Theatre and Associate Professor of Dance at Butler
University. He is well known as a choreographer, but
his interests extend beyond the creation of dances to
the collecting of historical documents and works of art
related to his profession. He has admirably
accumulated a tremendous visual record reminiscent
of many of the known extensive collections in this
country. The Theatre and Music Collections of the
Museum of the City of New York, The New York
Public Library Dance Collection, and the Spreckels
Dance Collection of the Fine Arts Museum of San
Francisco are important examples in public
institutions. Mr. Verdak's travels as a dancer with the
Ballet Russe de Monte Carlo give him a sound
perspective for the development of his collection.
Traveling and meeting artists brought him in close
contact with many of the historical figures reflected in
this exhibition *Eras of the Dance.*

The collection was first brought to our attention by
Audrey Gryder and the exhibition has been in the
planning stages for over a year. Subsequently, other
members of the staff visited Mr. Verdak in Indiana. He
allowed us complete freedom to study, to examine
numerous storage areas, and to make important notes
which helped us develop a cohesive concept of the
show.

From these meetings, we have selected 165 works
from approximately 800 sheets as the core of the
exhibition which is divided into nine sections.
Beginning with Early Theatre and Dance, the show
highlights important dance periods including the
Romantic Ballet and Diaghilev's Ballets Russes. Print
connoisseurs will delight in the material as much of it
is reflective of some of the best graphic production. For
example, François Chereau's engraving of Louis
Pécour and the wonderful line drawings of Isadora
Duncan by Abraham Walkowitz parallel the well-
known styles of Hogarth and Picasso. Richard Doyle's
pencil drawing entitled "Polka" is certainly as striking
and complex as much of Reginald Marsh's work.
Although these and other stylistic affinities are

isolated, they do focus our attention on a tremendous amount of graphic production which has not been fully explored by scholars.

From volumes of books and manuscripts, we have chosen to exhibit striking examples from the collection. Although limited by available space, we have included two important backdrops, one by Eugene Berman for the production *The Devil's Holiday* and the other by Salvador Dali for the ballet *Bacchanale*.

For the Montgomery Museum's installation, we enlisted the services of Douglas-Scott Goheen of Centerline Scenic Studios of Phoenix, Arizona who was asked to transform four galleries into a theatrical setting for the installation of the exhibition. In one instance, this involved a major lighting and stage design for the display of the Dali backdrop. This was necessary to allow Museum visitors a participatory experience by changing lighting effects through the operation of our dimmer board. American Stage Lighting, Inc. of New York provided the Museum with complete theatre lighting, booms, footlights, et cetera, which gives us a complete theatrical capability for our presentation. The Montgomery Performing Arts Company, Dance Department, will provide personnel to conduct improvisational workshops on the stage with the assistance of Betsy Brown from our staff. Ron Roth, State Museum Coordinator, and Claire Stevenson, Acting Curator of Education, have coordinated these important educational activities with Montgomery schools.

The generous assistance, encouragement, and advice of Mr. George Verdak must be graciously acknowledged as his scholarly remarks have added tremendously to our publication. Having very little time between his own productions, he flew to Montgomery to help us with last minute clarifications.

Diane J. Gingold has attended to the logistics of the exhibition, documented much of the collection, and compiled the entries for the catalog. I want to thank Ted James as he has admirably overseen the

installation at the Montgomery Museum requiring coordination between city departments. We would never have made our press deadline without the capable assistance of Patti Jordan who endlessly typed volumes of material.

We are particularly pleased that the show will travel to the Huntsville Museum of Art. Director Tom Bowles and members of his fine staff have shown a genuine interest in the exhibition early in its development.

It is with a deep sense of personal pride that the Montgomery Museum has organized an exhibition uniting the visual and performing arts in a truly educational style. We sincerely hope the show will be "Sold out."

Henry Flood Robert, Jr.
Director
Montgomery Museum of Fine Arts

Foreword

Like Mr. Field's fatal glass I bought a book in the mid-1930s. It cost me my lunch money for a number of days, the buying habit stuck fast, and the collecting process became progressively easier.

When I toured with the Ballet Russe de Monte Carlo, I hardly realized I was also seeing the last of the store-front bookmen who disappeared rapidly after the War. It was while visiting them that I frequently saw our company manager George Ford, himself an author, the grandson of Joseph Jefferson, and a member of the distinguished family who owned Ford's Theater in Washington.

He was collecting theatrical material to be housed at William and Mary College in his family's name, an idea I thought remarkably altruistic, "life enhancing" as Berenson says, and especially so when contrasted against the ephemeral nature of work in the theatre.

Ford's example gave me an inkling of the positive direction collecting could take even though I had no William and Mary in mind, long before I began to teach history of dance which made all the books and pictures even more immediate and fascinating.

With a point of view established, my holdings began to take on some proportion and dominated every living quarter I ever had as it still does. The theatrical specialists Samuel Hume (the friend of Appia and Gordon Craig, later founder of *Theater Arts* magazine), the scholarly Ifan Kyrle Fletcher in London, the charming Mme. Zlatin in Paris all supplied me with endless items and were always considerate to a fault when money matters arose.

When the unities of time, place, and finances stabilized, I was able to consider acquiring other collections and items in bulk: the Cortesi collection, the library of Cecil Hopkinson (a Diaghilev enthusiast and music historian), portions of the estate of Michel Fokine, plus generous gifts from the choreographer Ruth Page, and others.

A bare few months before this catalog was compiled, the musical library of Anna Pavlova and of the de Basil

Ballet tours came along to join the scores and orchestral materials of the London Ballet, the Pavley-Oukrainski Ballet, and the San Carlo Opera Ballet. This brought together for the first time a serious font of music for the ballet, the bulk of which was generally in manuscript form and vulnerable.

What a pleasure it is to be able to share some parts of the "iceberg," especially with friends in Montgomery where ballet has always been warmly and generously received.

I must thank all the kind people at the Montgomery Museum of Fine Arts who initiated the idea of the exhibit and who waded through mounds of dance material without flinching and with the conviction that all the disparate stuff would come together into some sort of homogenous whole.

George Verdak

10

Early Theatre and Dance

While the exhibit may not show any actual items before 1500, it should be known that there were serious writings on dance technique as early as 1300. Indeed, the development of western painting techniques, the early foundations of western musical science, and the development of dance technique into a recognizable and formal entity were all simultaneous. Dance was not a "come lately" art.

Recall that there were no formal theatres or public admission audiences until the middle of the 1600s and that there were many social restrictions against being a public performer.

Costumes, adapted from heavy formal court regalia, were cumbersome, the heelless slipper was unknown, and the elaborate wig and mask were obligatory. Little wonder that dance technique was precious, small in scope, and that the upper body (the least-hampered half) was generally more eloquent than the lower.

1. Johann Théodore de Bry
   1561 - 1623
   or
   Johann Israel de Bry
   1570 - 1611
   Engraving
   $4^1/_2$ x $5^5/_8$ *

   A Social Dance.

   The art of dancing enjoyed a glorious revival during
   the Renaissance. Court dances were adapted from
   popular folk dances and in Italy were recommended
   by Castiglione in *The Courtier* as being suitable for a
   gentleman to practice in both public and private. In
   France Catherine de Médicis encouraged musicians
   and dancing masters to come to Paris to stage court
   spectacles. In England, the masque and antemasque
   were a prevalent form of court entertainment (see
   entries 13 and 15).

2. Jacques Callot
   1592 - 1635
   Etching
   $7^1/_2$ x 11

   The Combat at the Barrier. Illustration for a festival
   book containing a prose description and poetry by
   Henry Humbert published in Nancy, 1627.

   Jacques Callot, a famous artist in his own day,
   executed a significant number of etchings on theatrical
   subjects. As a printmaker for the Medici, he was
   required to make official visual records of court
   festivals and theatrical extravaganzas organized by the
   court and often staged at the ducal palaces. This
   etching from a festival book documents a courtly
   entertainment held in Nancy.

3. Giacomo Cavalein Torelli
   1604/1608 - 1678
   Engraving
   $8^1/_2$ x $11^5/_8$

   Unidentified production. Scenic design.

   Giacomo Torelli was one of the first professional scene
   painters. A native Venetian, he went to Paris in 1645 at
   the invitation of Cardinal Mazarin although one story
   relates that he moved to Paris after an assassination
   attempt was made by spectators who believed some of
   his mystifying tricks indicated collusion with the devil.
   In Paris, he introduced stage machinery which
   permitted rapid scene changing and allowed him to
   create some of the most complicated and grandiose
   designs of the century. When he retired to Italy in
   1667, his pupils continued his work.

* Dimensions are given in inches.
  Height precedes width.

Combat a la Barriere   Jac. Callot In. et fec.

2

7

4. Ludovico Burnacini
    1636 - 1707
    Engraving
    $12^{1}/_{8}$ x $16^{7}/_{8}$

    Unidentified production. Scenic design.

    Like many other Renaissance artists, Ludovico
    Burnacini continued a family tradition, that is, both
    Ludovico and his father Giovanni were Viennese
    scenic designers and architects. As the popularity of
    the theatrical arts spread throughout Italy, the designs
    for stage, scenery, and costume became more elaborate
    and baroque. Burnacini, court architect for Leopold I of
    Vienna, was responsible for some of the masterpieces
    of his time.

5. Matthew Küsel
    after Ludovico Burnacini
    1636 - 1707
    Engraving
    $10^{3}/_{8}$ x $17^{3}/_{8}$

    Unidentified production. Scenic design.

    See entry 4.

6. Ludovico Burnacini
    1636 - 1707
    Engraving
    $11^{3}/_{8}$ x $17^{5}/_{8}$

    Unidentified production. Scenic design.

    See entry 4.

7. Ludovico Burnacini
    1636 - 1707
    Engraving
    $10^{1}/_{2}$ x $17^{5}/_{8}$

    Unidentified production. Scenic design.

    See entry 4.

8a.   Gerard Scotin
      1643(?) - 1715
      after Claude Gillot
      1673 - 1732
      Engraving
      $4^5/_8$ x $7^1/_2$

      Amadis by Jean Baptiste Lully. Scenic design for
      Prologue.

  b. Engraving
      $4^1/_2$ x $7^3/_4$

      Amadis. Scenic design for Act I.

  c. Engraving
      $4^5/_8$ x $7^5/_8$

      Amadis. Scenic design for Act II.

Jean Baptist Lully (1632 - 1687) was Florentine by
birth but is known for his career as composer, violinist,
and dancer for the French court in the service of Louis
XIV. He was influential in the creation of the
Académie Royale de la Musique of which he assumed
the directorship in 1672. During this period, he
established the opera-ballet in which music and
dancing shared equally with the dramatic action.
Among those with whom he collaborated were
Moliere, Racine, and the designer Jean Bérain (see
entry 16).

15

8c

9a. Gerard Scotin
1643(?) - 1715
after Claude Gillot
1673 - 1732
Engraving
$4^3/_4$ x $7^7/_8$

Thesée by Jean Baptiste Lully. Scenic design.

b. Engraving
$4^1/_2$ x $7^5/_8$

Thesée. Scenic design for Act II.

c. Engraving
$4^5/_8$ x $7^5/_8$

Thesée. Scenic design for Act V.

The recorded career of Claude Gillot began with his appointment as an associate of the Royal Academy in 1710 and his subsequent appointment as Director of Costumes and Decoration at the Opéra in 1715. He is known for his theatrical designs and for his genre painting and etchings which frequently depicted figures from the Italian *commedia dell'arte*.

10a-f. Unknown artist
Engraving
$13^1/_4$ x $17^1/_4$

Unidentified production. Scenic designs for six individual sets.

The elaborate scenic designs of the seventeenth century required the coordinated effort of painters, architects, engineers, and decorators. Opera, for the most part based on ancient Greek tragedy and myth, was the predominant theatrical form. Although operas were generally written for special occasions, their popularity led to the opening of the first opera-house for the general public in Venice in 1637. The engravings in this exhibition probably were published in commemorative volumes which illustrated the principle scenes for important productions. These volumes documented the history of seventeenth century theatre for both the immediate audience and future generations.

10

10c

11. Filippo Suchielli
Engraving
9³/₄ x 14

Unidentified production. Scenic design.

This engraving illustrates the use of stage machinery that simulates flight through the air. The use of the crane was introduced by the Greeks to allow the arrival and departure of divine figures. The expression *deus ex machina,* which originally referred to the arrival of a god by means of a crane to decide the final outcome of a theatrical performance, came to signify a dramatic device to bring a problem or action to a swift and often contrived conclusion.

11

12. Giulio Parigi
1571 - 1635
Etching
8¹/₈ x 11

A Water Ballet for a production for the Wedding of the
Prince of Tosca, 1608.

The Florentine Giulio Parigi was a master organizer
and designer of courtly productions of the sixteenth
and seventeenth centuries. It is probable that he was
the teacher of Callot whose etchings and drawings
recorded the designs of his master. These spectacles
were executed primarily for the powerful Medici
grand dukes.

12

Early Ballet

It took someone of enormous influence to pull together all the resources of theatrical dance and send it down a productive path less free of the technical restrictions and social prejudicies that barred its progress.

The catalyst was Louis XIV, an enthusiastic dancer himself who appeared in ballet performances until he was past thirty.

Receptive to the advice of his gifted ballet masters, he gave them their own guild, charged them to devise a common language of movement terminology and to find a way to notate dancing.

By his own participation and by formal fiat, he declared that dancing in public, as a professional, would carry no social stigma or incur any forfeit. The way was free for the first generation of real professionals.

13. Jaspar Isac
    d. 1654
    after Unknown Artist
    Engraving
    $9^1/_8$ x $7^3/_8$

    Comus, masque by John Milton. First performed at Ludlow Castle, 1634.

    The masque, a variation of the Italian masquerade and the French *ballet de cour,* was a courtly allegorical or mythological play including songs, speeches, dance, and poetry performed by members of the court and nobility. By 1512, it was introduced to England at the Court of Henry VIII and two decades later was introduced to France by Catherine de Médicis. In England, composers of masques included the outstanding poets Ben Jonson (1572 - 1637) and John Milton (1608 - 1674). Inigo Jones (1573 - 1652), one of England's great architects, designed scenery for these productions. The performance of these compositions was both a literary and social event.

14. French School
    c. 1650
    Engraving
    $7^3/_4$ x 12

    Habit de Masque.

    See entry 13.

15. French School
    c. 1650
    Engraving
    $8^1/_8$ x 12

    Monsieur du Moulin in the costume of a grotesque.

    The antemasque was an innovation by Jonson which introduced the grotesque or antic element to the performance which preceded the masque proper. The antemasque differed from the masque in that it was performed by professionals instead of the lords and ladies of the court. Grotesque or antic dancing had been seen previously but in the form of the antemasque it was one of England's greatest contributions to theatrical dancing. Monsieur du Moulin who appears in this engraving in the costume of a grotesque was one of the earliest professional male dancers.

16. Jean Bérain the Elder
1640 - 1711
Engraving
7³/₄ x 12

Monsieur du Moulin in the costume of a country man.

From 1673 until his death, Jean Bérain was associated with the Académie Royale de Danse established in Paris in 1661 by Louis XIV to instruct courtiers in dancing, create court ballets, and prepare professional ballet masters and choreographers. For about ten years he designed only costumes, including some for the King's ballet appearances. In 1681, however, he began to design sets. In this manner he influenced non-theatrical ornamentation of rooms and furniture. His son Jean succeeded him but failed to equal his father's talent.

17a. School of Bérain
c. 1650
Gouache
17¹/₈ x 11⁷/₈

Unindentified production. Costume design for male performer.

b. Gouache
17¹/₈ x 11⁷/₈

Unindentified production. Costume design for female performer.

In France, the work of Jean Bérain the Elder epitomized costume designs of the Louis XIV era. Emphasis was placed on style, and both realism and archaeological reconstructions bowed to the dictates of the personal interpretation of Bérain. Jean Bérain the Younger and the School of Bérain continued to copy and produce designs in the style of the master.

18. François Chereau
1680 - 1729
after R. Fourniere
Engraving
16³/₄ x 11⁵/₈

Portrait of Louis Pécour.

Louis Pécour (1655 - 1729) was the first *premier danseur* for the Royal Academy of Dance founded in 1671 by Louis XIV as L'Académie de Musique et de Danse and known today as the Paris Opéra. Later, he became its second ballet master after the resignation of Pierre Beauchamp. He is credited with the creation of the minuet and he was the first to use dance notation which he introduced in his book *Chorégraphie ou l'Art d'Ecrire la Danse.* As a dancer, he was notable for precision, grace, and his *elevation,* the ability to jump high in the air.

Du Moulin en habit de Paysan
Dansant a L'Opera

Du feu de son génie il anima la Danse;
Aux beaux jours de la Grèce il sut la rappeler,
Et recouvrant par lui leur antique éloquence
Les Gestes et les Pas aprirent à parler.

par B. Imbert.

Guerin del.

B. Roger Sculp.

19. Barthélemy Joseph Fulcran Roger
     1767 - 1841
     after Pierre-Narcisse Guérin
     1774 - 1833
     Engraving
     6$^7/_8$ x 4$^1/_2$

     Portrait of Jean Georges Noverre.

     Jean Georges Noverre (1727 - 1810), dancer,
     choreographer, and ballet master, wrote the great
     critical text *Lettres sur la Danse et sur les Ballets*
     (1760). He advanced the idea that the elements of
     ballet, dancing, painting, pantomime, and music,
     should be unified into a dramatic whole. He advised:
     "Children of Terpsichore . . . renounce
     overcomplicated steps . . . abandon grimaces to study
     sentiments . . . study how to make your gestures
     noble . . . away with those lifeless masks . . . a
     well-composed ballet is a living picture of the passions,
     manners, habits, ceremonies, and customs of all
     nations of the globe . . . "

20. John Miller
     active c. 1760
     after Unknown Artist
     Engraving
     7$^1/_4$ x 4$^3/_8$

     Portrait of Gaetan Vestris, Senior. Reproduced in
     London Magazine, 1781.

     In 1751, Gaetan Vestris (1729 - 1808) became *premier
     danseur* of the Opéra and ten years later was
     appointed ballet master. Vestris' outstanding ability as
     a dancer was equalled only by his arrogance and
     conceit which caused several conflicts within the
     Opéra during his lifetime. In Stuttgart he worked with
     Noverre. Vestris was one of the first dancers to
     abandon the mask to reveal an excellent talent for
     mime.

21. La Fosse
     after L.C. de Mormantelle
     Colored engraving
     10$^1/_2$ x 7$^1/_2$

     Portrait of Louise-Madeleine Lany.

     Little is known about Louise-Madeleine Lany (b.
     1733). She was the sister of the Opéra ballet master
     Jean Lany, a *danseuse* at the Opéra and admired by
     Noverre for her beauty, speed, and precise technique.

22. Jules Porreau
     active 1845 - 1866
     after Unknown Artist
     Engraving
     8$^1/_2$ x 5$^1/_4$

     Portrait of Marie Madeleine Guimard.

     Marie Madeleine Guimard (1743 - 1816) became a
     member of the Comédie Française *corps de ballet* at
     the age of fifteen and made her debut at the Paris
     Opéra in 1762. She is remembered not as a creator of
     specific roles but for her interpretive ability in
     character and mime roles in which she excelled. She
     owned a sumptuous home decorated by Jean-Honore
     Fragonard and Jacques Louis David. After her
     marriage to Jean Etienne Despréaux in 1789, she
     retired from the stage.

23. Philippe Trière
     1756 - 1815
     after Jean Etienne Despréaux
     1748 - 1820
     Engraving
     7$^5/_8$ x 4$^3/_4$

     Profile silhouette of Jean Etienne Despréaux.
     Frontispiece of *Mes Passe-temps* by Despréaux.

     Jean Etienne Despréaux (1748 - 1820) was a dancer
     with a promising career at the Paris Opéra until a foot
     injury caused him to retire. He continued his artistic
     career as a violinist, ballet master, poet, and stage
     manager. After his marriage to the prominent dancer
     Marie Guimard in 1789, they retired to Montmartre
     where they continued to pursue their interest in dance.

24. Unknown Artist
    c. 1750
    Watercolor
    10 x 7⅝

Portrait of Mlle. Auretti.

The heeled shoes and long skirt were characteristic of the female dance costume until Marie Camargo (1710 - 1770) shortened the skirt to midway between the ankle and the knee. Already freed from the mask, and now freed from long skirts, movement became more complicated which led to the invention of new steps.

25. English School
    Engraving
    5½ x 3⅞

Portrait of Auguste Vestris, Junior. Reproduced in *London Magazine*, 1781.

Auguste Vestris (1760 - 1842) was considered by his father Gaetan to be the *Le Dieu de la Danse*. He explained that it was possible for Auguste to be more skillful than himself because, "Gaetan is his father — an advantage nature denied me." Auguste, an outstanding dancer of classic ballet and character parts, was known for his *entrechats*, pirouettes, and elevation. In 1816, he retired from the stage to teach at the Opéra where his students included Fanny Elssler, Charles Didelot, and Jules Perrot.

26. Abraham Teniers
    1629 - 1670
    Engraving
    9 x 11⅞

Unidentified production. Scenic design.

The scenic designs of the seventeenth and eighteenth centuries reflected parallel interests in the other fine arts. Chinoiserie was first introduced to Europe as a result of the travels of Marco Polo in the thirteenth century. It reappeared in various forms during the following centuries as a representation of the exotic. In this engraving, Teniers recorded the Oriental influence in theatrical costume.

27. F.M. Francia
active mid-17th century
after Domenico Mauro
Engraving
11^1/$_2$ x 15

Hercules at Thebes. Scenic design.

During the Renaissance, the revival of interest in
classical art forms was evident in all phases of culture.
Neoclassic architectural structures were constructed
for scenic designs and pastiches of sculpture graced
the stage (see entry 221). Similarly, Greek myth
provided the basis for many theatrical and ballet
stories such as *Hercules at Thebes,* the production
for which this scenic design was created.

27

28. Simon Fokke
1712 - 1784
Engraving
$7^3/_4$ x $11^5/_8$

Unidentified production. Scenic design.

In this gala scene, appropriate lighting was provided by candle chandeliers. By the eighteenth century, stage lighting had reached a fairly high degree of sophistication in Italy so that France and England adapted some of the Italian inventions. Footlights, overhead lighting, and colored lights were utilized to create atmospheric effects.

29a. Unknown Artist
Engraving
$5^3/_4$ x $10^5/_8$

Unidentified production. Scenic design.

b. Engraving
$5^1/_2$ x 8

Unidentified production. Scenic design.

These two engravings illustrate the early development of legs and borders, narrow strips of painted cloth used to mask the top and sides of the stage from the auditorium audience. Cloudings, or borders of clouds that could be drawn off the stage by hooked poles, had been used earlier (see entry 11).

30. James Caldwell
b. 1739
after Robert Adam
1728 - 1792
Engraving
13 x $17^1/_8$

Inside view of the Ball-room in a Pavilion erected for a Fête Champêtre in the Garden of the Earl of Derby at the Oaks in Surry, the 9th of June, 1774.

Dance continued to be a popular form of entertainment for the nobility in the eighteenth century. Robert Adam, a prominent British architect who designed neoclassic country houses, specially built this structure for a garden party given by the Earl of Derby in 1774.

De Vrede, als uit den hemel nederdalende, vertoond, by het water openen van den Amsteld. Schouwburg A.º 1749 in het Zinnespel **Leeuwendaal hersteld door de Vrede.**

28

Alcmena. deß Thebanischen Fürsten Gemahlin
Sie hatten diesen geheyrathet, daß er ihres Bruders Todt rächen
solte: In währenden diesen, Feld-Zug ward Jupiter in sie verliebt,
nahm des Amptrijons gestalt an sich, kam in einer Nacht zu Ih-
ro machte diese Nacht 3. mahl 24. Stunden lang, damit er Zeit genug hätte
und nicht entecket würde. Obwolen nun Alcmena mit Iphiclo schwä-
ger gienge, kam doch noch Herculus dar zu, und gebahr sie beyde auf ein mahl.

Ein Heydnischer Priester sein Nahme heist Coribantes von Cijbele wurde von Numa Pompilio
vor die Römer mit vielen ceremonien gestifftet u. geehret, diese waren zu dem Ewigen feuer welches
bey den Vestalischen Jungfrawen breñte müste auf sehen, wañ diese das feuer aus löschen liessen: wurden sie von
den Priester hart gestrafft, und dorffte solches nicht wider angezündet werde als durch der Sonen strahlen, die-
ser Priester müste weiß angelegt seyn. sein Kleid Albagenennet, über dieses müste er einen farbigen Ober-Rock
mit einem ehrinen brust blatt, welches sich hernach in silber u. Gold verändert, dieses wird Chasuble
ode Casel genennet. Zum opfer bedeckten sie die Köpfe mit einer decke, Amictus genennet.
Sie befielen ihre Götter mit ungleichen bewegungen, bald gegen Aufgang bald gegen Nider-
der Sonnen an, und tanckten vor dem Altare mit Allerley Geberden diese Priester habe
den Jupiter erzogen welch ihnen von der Cybelle anvertraut worden.

31b   31c

31a. Messebrenter
active first half 18th century
Colored engraving
$12\frac{1}{4}$ x $7\frac{1}{4}$

Castor and Pollux by Jean Philippe Rameau. First
performed with Gaetan Vestris at the Académie
Royale, Paris, 1772. Costume design for a male
warrior.

  b. Colored engraving
12 x 7

Alcemena. Costume design for female performer.

  c. Colored engraving
$11\frac{3}{4}$ x $7\frac{1}{4}$

Unidentified German ballet, 1723. Costume design for
male performer.

The costumes of the early ballet continued to be
elaborately decorative, ornamental, and negligible in
historical accuracy. Movement was still controlled and
stylized as dictated by the costume.

32a. François Chauveau
1613 - 1676
after Henri Gissey
1621 - 1673

Colored engraving
$12\frac{1}{4}$ x $10\frac{1}{2}$

Grand Carrousel, 1662. Design for Roman drummers.

  b. Colored engraving
$12\frac{1}{4}$ x $10\frac{1}{2}$

Design for two young men on horseback.

The *Grand Carrousel* or *Carrousel de Louis XIV* was
an outdoor spectacle ballet presented in Paris.
Chauveau recorded the elaborate Roman costumes
designed for the noblemen on horseback and others
who participated in the mock-tournament. This
particular production, designed for the King by his
court designer Gissey, became a model for similar
extravagant fêtes throughout the continent.

32b

33. Le Couteur (?)
     c. 1775
     Pencil drawing
     $16^{1}/_{2}$ x $21^{1}/_{8}$

Le Menuet de la Cour.

The minuet was a courtly dance introduced in France
during the reign of Louis XIV. It was derived from the
sixteenth century *basse danse* in which the dancer's
feet barely left the ground. The minuet, a stately and
elegant dance in 3/4 time was described in detail by
Pierre Rameau in his well known book *Le Maître a
Danser* (1725, see entry 125). The *Menuet de la Cour*
was one type of the dance.

34. Unknown Artist
     Wash drawing
     $5^{3}/_{4}$ x 8

Sketch of three eighteenth century dancers.

34

33

Pre-Romantic Ballet

Noverre, the performer of the previous era, had decreed the end of hoops, of masks and wigs, of heeled shoes, and the gentle tyranny of the classic dance forms.

While he did a great deal of this work during his own career, it fell to Salvatore Vigano, in the next generation, to stand back, assess the worth of Noverre, and to incorporate all the new findings in his own great ballets.

Via Gluck, music had become less formal. Vigano went directly to Beethoven who wrote the lengthy "Prometheus" ballet for him.

Sanquirico, the giant of the scene designers, had shucked the sterile symmetry of the eras past and gave Vigano lush and full-blown décors that were to usher in the even more esoteric novelties of the Romantic era.

Costume design, with continual prodding, began to be more suited to action, and experiments were made with light Graeco-Roman tunics which gave all parts of the body an increased mobility.

35. C. Zucchi
after Alessandro Sanquirico
1777 - 1849
Engraving
$13^1/_8$ x $15^3/_4$

Il Conte d'Essex. Choreography by Gaetano Gioja. Performed at La Scala, Milan, 1818. Scenic design.

As was mentioned previously, scenic design reflected contemporary fashionable artistic styles. The English enthusiasm for neo-Gothic design was exemplified in Strawberry Hill, a "little Gothic castle" built by Horace Walpole, complete with stained glass windows, pointed windows, and painted fretwork. A similar Gothic atmosphere for the theatre was created and recorded in this engraving of a Queen's chambers.

36. C. Sanquirico
after Alessandro Sanquirico
1777 - 1849
Engraving
$13^5/_8$ x $16^1/_2$

Pelia e Mileto. Choreography by Salvatore Taglioni. Performed at La Scala, Milan, 1827.

Italian artists were responsible for a major portion of the operatic and ballet masterpieces of this period. Alessandro Sanquirico collaborated with Salvatore Vigano to create spectacular ballets for La Scala. The settings were oriented toward neoclassic architecture and, as illustrated in this engraving, the space was often crowded with architecture, figures, and stage devices.

37. Alessandro Sanquirico
1777 - 1849
Color lithograph
$8^1/_8$ x 12

Gengis Khan. Scenic design.

This color lithograph is indicative of the popularity of Sanquirico. Only the best-known artists would have their designs reproduced in large and luxurious lithographs for sale to the public.

38. Alessandro Sanquirico
1777 - 1849
Watercolor
$8^3/_8$ x $10^7/_8$

Unidentified production by Antonio Cortesi. Design for a carrousel.

See entry 36.

39. David de Boschi
Gouache and ink
$10^7/_8$ x $16^1/_2$

Unidentified ballet by Antonio Cortesi. Scenic design.

This scenic design exemplifies the typical neoclassic architectural setting derived from Renaissance architecture. Atmospheric effect was created in this design by the use of a blue wash.

40. Jean Prud'hon
b. 1778
after Sébastien Coéure
b. 1778
Colored engraving
$13^1/_4$ x 10

Monsieur Paul in *Clary, the Maid of Milan.*

The costume worn by the dancer in this engraving demonstrates the development of the male ballet costume. The shortened trousers which revealed more of the leg and tights permitted greater freedom of movement. Similarly, the female costume was shortened by Marie Camargo enabling her to execute more complicated steps with greater vivacity (see entry 24). Male ballet dancers continued to wear this type of costume for the remainder of the century (see entry 72).

41. François Levasseur (?)
active first half 19th century
Lithograph
$9^3/_4$ x $6^7/_8$

Signor Samingo and Madame Brugnoli in the ballet *L'Anneau Magique.*

This lithograph is one of the earliest prints which illustrates the female dancer on *pointes* (toe). Eighteen twenty-one was the date of the first known print showing a dancer on *pointes,* the Romantic ballet's outstanding contribution to dance technique.

42. Hélène Feillet
active first half 19th century
Color lithograph
$12^1/_8$ x $9^1/_2$

Mimi Dupuis and Mazurier in *La Neige.*

43c

43a. E. Vigano
active first half 19th century
Watercolor
$10^1/_8$ x $8^1/_2$

Unidentified ballet by Antonio Cortesi. Costume design for Beatrice Tenda.

b. Watercolor
$9^1/_4$ x $6^1/_4$

Unidentified ballet by Antonio Cortesi. Costume design for elderly courtier.

c. Watercolor
$10^3/_8$ x $7^7/_8$

Unidentified ballet by Antonio Cortesi. Transformation costume design.

d. Watercolor
$9^1/_4$ x $6^1/_4$

Unindentified ballet by Antonio Cortesi. Costume design for the children of the Duke of Borganza.

e. Watercolor
$9^3/_8$ x $6^1/_8$

Unidentified Scottish ballet by Antonio Cortesi. Costume design for male performer.

f. Watercolor
$8^3/_8$ x $6^1/_4$

Unidentified ballet by Antonio Cortesi. Costume design for female comic performer.

g. Watercolor
$9^1/_4$ x $6^3/_4$

Unidentified ballet by Antonio Cortesi. Warrior costume design for Clotario.

The family name Vigano is notable in dance history for Salvatore Vigano (1769 - 1821), an outstanding Italian dancer and choreographer. Research has not been able to document any relationship of E. Vigano to Salvatore Vigano or the Vigano family, a family involved with dance for several generations. These costume sketches by E. Vigano are typical of the period.

44a. Alessandro Sanquirico
1777 - 1849
Watercolor
$8^1/_4$ x $6^1/_2$

Unidentified ballet by Antonio Cortesi. Costume design for male Greek figure.

b. Watercolor
$8^5/_8$ x $5^5/_8$

Unidentified ballet by Antonio Cortesi. Costume design for lawyer.

c. Watercolor
$8^3/_8$ x $6^1/_8$

Unidentified ballet by Antonio Cortesi. Costume design for page.

These costume designs illustrate the diversified talent of Alessandro Sanquirico (see entries 35-38). Most of the original sketches by the artist have been preserved at La Scala, Milan. These sheets are several of the rare examples found in the United States.

45a. Adamo Tadolini
1788 - 1868
Watercolor
$8^1/_8$ x $5^1/_8$

Unidentified biblical ballet by Antonio Cortesi. Costume for royal page in the Hebrew court.

b. Watercolor
$7^3/_8$ x $5^3/_4$

Unidentified biblical ballet by Antonio Cortesi. Costume for Hebrew priest.

c. Watercolor
$8^1/_8$ x $5^7/_8$

Unidentified biblical ballet by Antonio Cortesi. Costume for Hebrew elder.

46. Phillippe Jacques de Loutherbourg
1740 - 1812
Wash drawing
$8^5/_8$ x 5

Grotesque figure, perhaps a theatrical caricature study for one of the figures painted in *The Rainbow*, 1778.

Phillippe Jacques de Loutherbourg, a Frenchman who worked in England from the year 1771, advanced the use of romantic landscape rather than architectural settings for scenic designs. He worked primarily for the Drury Lane Theatre designing scenes for pantomimes and similar entertainments. His inventions of transparent scenery and ''cut-out'' scenery contributed to the diversity of the stage picture.

47

47. French School
Color engraving
9³/₈ x 12⁷/₈

Zephyr and Flora ("Les Coulisses de l'Opéra") by Charles Louis Didelot. First performed in London, 1796.

In the foreground of this scene from Didelot's most famous ballet, is a typical figure of an acrobat male dancer taking the part of an animal. Jules Perrot, one of the greatest male dancers of the Romantic era (see entry 57), began his ballet career as a mime in French provincial theaters.

48. George Cruikshank
1792 - 1878
Colored engraving
10 x 14¹/₈

Longitude and Latitude of St. Petersburgh, 1813.

The Elizabethan artist found fertile material for caricature and satire in the contemporary dancing craze of his era. Dancing schools abounded in London where intricate and fashionable dances imported from France were taught. The popularity of dance continued in the succeeding centuries, and likewise continued to be the subject of the satirical artist. This engraving by Cruikshank, one of the leading caricaturists of the nineteenth century, exemplifies this artistic form.

49. Krakskievic
Color engraving
9⁷/₈ x 14

The Hambourg Waltz with Characteristic Sketches of Family Dancing!, 1818.

The craze for social dancing reached new heights at the Congress of Vienna in 1814 and 1815 which was dubbed "The Dancing Congress."

50. English School
Engraving
9³/₄ x 13⁷/₈

The Favorite Instrument, The Fife, 1821.

See entry 48.

51. English School
Color lithograph
4¹/₂ x 6⁵/₈

Scene in the Green Room of the Opera, Kings Theatre, London, 1822.

See entry 48.

LONGITUDE & LATITUDE of St PETERSBURGH.

Publd May 18th 1813 by H. Humphrey, St James's Street

G. Cruikshank fect

Romantic Ballet

As in no other period prior, the Romantic dancers were becoming ready technically and pictorially to use dance as a theatrical medium of mood and passion.

Led by the geniuses of Romantic literature, Gautier, Heine, Novalis, Funck-Bretano, Hoffman, dance took off on an extravagant quarter century swing which did not wind down until the middle of the nineteenth century.

The introduction of toe technique and of acrobatic adagio made more plausible the treatment of a variety of romantic librettos peopled with a whole new strata of exotic stage creatures.

Sylphs, naiads, wilis, nixes, dryads, hamadryads were typical categories of half-human characters (mostly taken by women) that peopled the stage of the Romantic ballet.

The male disappeared farther and farther into the background before this onslaught of twilight creatures and finally, the vein of fantasy completely exhausted, the Romantic ballet collided with the opera and began to lose ground.

52. François-Séraphin Delpech
1728 - 1825
after Zéphirin-Félix-Jean-Marius Belliard
b. 1798
Engraving
$19^1/_8$ x $12^1/_8$

Portrait of Marie Taglioni.

Marie Taglioni (1804 - 1884) is the ballerina most symbolic of the Romantic era. Descended from a dynasty of dancers dating from her grandfather, she received her ballet training from her father Philippe Taglioni who also choreographed the ballet for her debut in 1822 at the Hoftheater, Vienna. Taglioni's unique style was a combination of gracefulness of attitude, lightness of step, a phenomenal elevation, and an indefinable ethereal and spiritual quality. Toward the end of her life, poverty forced her to return to teaching dance in Paris and London.

53. Richard James Lane
1800 - 1872
after Alfred-Edward Chalon
1780 - 1860
Lithograph
15 x $10^1/_4$

La Sylphide by Adolphe Nourrit. Choreography by Phillippe Taglioni. First performed by Marie Taglioni at the Paris Opéra, Paris, 1832.

La Sylphide was created for Marie Taglioni by her father Philippe. Greek legends and classical themes were abandoned for a new romanticism. The new style of choreography was the epitome of fantasy, and juxtaposed the real and the supernatural. Eugene Lami introduced a new style of costume consisting of a tight fitting bodice which left the neck and shoulders bare, a bell shaped skirt that reached midway between the knee and the ankle, and pale pink tights and satin shoes. The costume and the plot of *La Sylphide* were to serve repeatedly as ballet models.

54. Unknown Artist
Color engraving
$10^1/_4$ x $17^1/_2$

Fan cover showing Marie Taglioni in seven different national costumes. Identifiable are Nathalie, the Swiss milkmaid (left to right, no. 1) and La Bayadère (no. 6).

After Marie Taglioni's appearance in *La Sylphide,* she became the "rage of Paris." Her popularity was witnessed in the production of lithographs and prints depicting the ballerina in a variety of roles as in this fan cover.

Marie Taglioni

55. Jules Peyre
active mid-19th century
after Unknown Artist
Lithograph
10 x 7

Portrait of Fanny Elssler.

The ballet style of Fanny Elssler (1810 - 1884), Taglioni's most serious rival, was distinctly opposite to that of Taglioni. Elssler's dancing, according to Gautier, was "more human, more appealing to the senses," whereas Taglioni was the essence of "aerial and virginal grace." Elssler made her debut in her native Vienna in 1822; her debut at the Paris Opéra did not occur until 1834. The years 1840 to 1842 were spent in the United States where she was enthusiastically received by President Van Buren (Congress adjourned each time she danced in Washington), the press, and the American public. She performed very little after her great triumphs in Russia and retired comfortably in Vienna.

56. Alexandre Lacouchie
active 19th century
after Jean-Baptiste Barré
1807 - 1877

Colored lithograph
10 x 6¹/₄

Fanny Elssler in a Cachucha costume, after a statue by Barré.

Fanny Elssler introduced character dances of national origins into many of her ballets of which the Spanish *cachucha* is an example. She first performed this Spanish dance in Paris in 1836 in the pantomime ballet *Le Diable Boiteux*. The original costume, preserved in the Museum of the City of Vienna, was pink and black, not yellow as colored in this lithograph.

57a. Alexandre Lacouchie
active 19th century
Color lithograph
11¹/₄ x 8¹/₄

Jules Perrot in an unidentified ballet.

b. Unknown Artist
Color lithograph
10¹/₂ x 6⁵/₈

Jules Perrot in the role of Alain in *La Filleule des Fées* by Vernoy de Saint-Georges and Perrot. Choreography by Perrot. First performed by Carlotta Grisi at the Paris Opéra, 1849.

Jules Joseph Perrot (1810 - 1892), a short man with ugly features, overcame his physical handicaps and the nineteenth century prejudice against male dancers to become in the words of Gautier, "the greatest dancer of our times." He began his career as a mime in provincial French theatres and made his ballet debut at the Paris Opéra at the age of twenty. In 1845, he choreographed the famous *Pas de Quatre* danced by Taglioni, Grisi, Cerrito, and Grahn at Her Majesty's Theatre, London. He subsequently staged productions throughout Europe and in St. Petersburg.

58a. Unknown Artist
Lithograph
9¹/₈ x 7¹/₄

Mlle. Céleste in an unidentified production.

b. Mlle. Céleste
Autographed note

Céleste Keppler (1811 - 1882), known as Mlle. Céleste, was a dancer familiar to the American audience. She toured the United States in 1827 and 1834, and in 1835 presented the first American performance of *La Sylphide*. After her retirement in 1874, she returned to Paris, her native city.

59.	Unknown Artist
	Color lithograph
	12^1/$_2$ x 9

	Pauline Duvernay in *Sleeping Beauty of the Woods*.

	Pauline Duvernay (1813 - 1894), a student of Auguste Vestris and Philippe Taglioni, attended the school of the Paris Opéra. After her Parisian debut in 1832, she appeared in London where she was applauded equally for her abilities as a ballerina and a fine interpretive actress. She danced for only five years before retiring from the stage. During the Romantic era, the interest in gossip and scandal, particularly about ballerinas, was at its height. Duvernay obligingly provided topics of conversation during her brief career with her lively escapades and flirtations.

60a.	Unknown Artist
	Engraving
	5 x 8

	Portrait of Lucile Grahn.

b.	Lucile Grahn
	Autographed note

	Lucile Grahn (1819 - 1907) was Danish by birth and made her debut at the age of ten in Denmark. After an argument with her ballet master Auguste Bournonville in 1839, she never danced again in Denmark; however, she achieved international fame and was particularly successful in Germany and Austria. After her retirement in 1856, she choreographed many opera-ballets.

61a.	Alexandre Lacouchie
	active 19th century
	Color lithograph
	10^5/$_8$ x 7^1/$_4$

	Carlotta Grisi in *Filleule des Fées* (see entry 57).

b.	Color lithograph
	10^5/$_8$ x 7

	Carlotta Grisi in *Diable à Quatre*.

	Carlotta Grisi (1819 - 1899), an Italian ballerina, studied voice in addition to dance. She made her debut at the Paris Opéra in *La Favorita* (see entry 65) in 1841, but is most famous for her creation of the title role in *Giselle* which she performed at the Opéra in the same year. In 1843 in *La Péri,* she introduced acrobatic adagio into classical ballet, and it is probable that she also was the first ballerina to dance in the boxed slipper. Grisi retired to Vienna at the age of thirty-five after dancing for three years at the St. Petersburg Imperial Theatre.

62a.	Auguste Hüsener
	1789 - 1877
	Engraving
	10^1/$_2$ x 4^1/$_4$

	Portrait of Fanny Cerrito.

b.	Fanny Cerrito
	Autographed note

	Fanny Cerrito (1821 - 1909) made her London debut at Her Majesty's Theatre, London, in 1840 and became an immediate critical success. When she danced in Paris, she was praised for her grace of poise and admirable ease of execution. Cerrito and Arthur Saint-Léon were married in 1845 and although they were separated in 1850, they continued to work together. A trip to Russia in 1855 marked the end of her career. During a performance a piece of scenery caught on fire and fell on the ballerina which caused heart injury necessitating her retirement from the stage.

63a.	Alexandre Lacouchie
	active 19th century
	Color lithograph
	10^1/$_2$ x 6^5/$_8$

	Fanny Cerrito in *Le Violin du Diable* by Arthur Saint-Léon. Choreography by Saint-Léon. First performed by Cerrito and Saint-Léon at the Paris Opera, 1849.

b.	Color lithograph
	10^1/$_2$ x 6

	Fanny Cerrito in *Pâquerette* by Théophile Gautier. Choreography by Saint-Léon. Performed by Cerrito at the Paris Opéra, 1851.

	Arthur Saint-Léon (1815? - 1870), husband of Fanny Cerrito for several years in the 1840s, was a choreographer, dancer, and violinist. His career as a choreographer began in 1847 when he staged the ballet *La Fille de Marbre* for Cerrito's debut at the Paris Opéra. In the production of *Le Violin du Diable* he demonstrated his abilities in all three areas. In 1859, he made his debut at the Imperial Theatre in St. Petersburg where he remained until 1869. During his lifetime, he staged ballets in all major European cities except Milan.

49

63b

64. Celestin François Nanteuil-Leboeuf
1813 - 1873
Lithograph
$9^3/_4$ x $12^3/_4$

Giselle by Vernoy de Saint-Georges, Théophile Gautier, and Jean Coralli. Choreography by Jules Perrot and Coralli. First performed by Carlotta Grisi and Lucien Petipa at the Paris Opéra, 1841. Music cover for piano quadrille composed by Musard.

A popular German legend by the poet Heinrich Heine provided the basic story for *Giselle,* a romantic tale about the peasant girl Giselle and her lover Count Albrecht. It enjoyed an immediate success and has frequently appeared on ballet programs throughout the world. The ballet was added to the repertoire of the Romantic ballerinas Elssler, Cerrito, and Grahn and in later years was danced by Anna Pavlova, Tamara Karsavina, and others.

65. English School
Lithograph
$13^1/_4$ x $9^5/_8$

Music cover for quadrille's from *L'Ange de Liside (La Favorita)* by Gaetano Donizetti. First performed by Lucien Petipa and Carlotta Grisi at the Paris Opéra, 1840. Performed by Marius Petipa and Grisi at the Theatre Royal, Drury Lane, London. Arranged for piano-forte by W. H. Montgomery.

Music covers of this period often reproduced scenes from popular ballets with the artists posed in characteristic roles. This particular cover was created for an English version of quadrilles from *La Favorita.* In nineteenth century Britain, the quadrille was a popular ballroom dance derived from eighteenth century French opera-ballets and adapted from the Parisian quadrille or cotillon. One of the peripheral values of the music cover print is that it occasionally shows us an interesting view of the scenery and of the additional characters who peopled the stage.

66. J. Brandard
1812 - 1863
Lithograph
$13^1/_8$ x $9^5/_8$

Music cover for *No. 1, The Original Mazurka,* composed by Jullien.

The composer Jullien, like the conductor Musard (see entry 64), became wealthy by publishing piano arrangements of popular ballet extracts and of social dances. J. Brandard, and A. E. Chalon (see entry 53) were two of the most prominent Victorian pictorial lithographers. The mazurka, a peasant dance originating in Poland in the sixteenth century, was popular in Germany, Paris, and London where it was often the concluding selection for court balls.

67. J. Brandard
1812 - 1863

Color lithograph
$13^3/_8$ x $9^3/_4$

Zouleika, a dance composed by Cellarius.

During the eighteenth and nineteenth centuries, special dance publications were issued which gave instructions for newly created dances. The Zouleika, a type of waltz and mazurka, was composed and titled by Cellarius for the purpose of public sale.

Second Empire Ballet and Victorian Ballet

The Paris Opéra continued to employ the best talent available, however, the ideas being developed did not equal its reputation. The exclusion of the male dancer left a lopsided feminine showcase which, more often than not, resulted in the succession of vapid, pretty pictures. In such a case, it is interesting to find that the debilitated dance scene was temporarily propped up with contributions by the other arts.

In France, the music of such interesting composers as Delibes, Lalo, and Messager held the ballet together briefly. In England, the Empire Theatre Ballet was eventually dominated by the fascinating but finicky designer C. Wilhelm.

68a. Unknown Artist
Wood engraving
$6^{5}/_{8}$ x $4^{3}/_{4}$

Emma Livry in *La Sylphide* (see entry 53).

b. Autographed letter

Emma Livry (1842 - 1863), the last of the Romantic ballerinas and the first outstanding French dancer in approximately two decades, was a protégée of Marie Taglioni whose influence was prominently visible. She made her debut at the Paris Opéra at the age of sixteen in *La Sylphide* and was enthusiastically acclaimed. The promising career of this artist was brought to a tragic end when her skirt caught fire at a rehearsal.

69. After a photograph by M. Benque
Photo reproduction
$10^{7}/_{8}$ x 8

Rosita Mauri in an unidentified Spanish ballet.

After the death of Emma Livry, many of the Paris Opéra's principal dancers came from countries other than France. The Spanish ballerina Rosita Mauri (1849 - 1923) was a leading dancer at the Teatro Barcelona before she made her debut at the Opéra in 1878. She remained on the stage until 1907 and after her retirement taught for an additional twelve years.

70. Marie-Alexandre Alophe
1812 - 1883
Color lithograph
$13^{1}/_{8}$ x 10

Zina Richard in *Marco Spada, ou La Fille du Bandit*, adapted from the comic opera *Marco Spada* by Mazilier. Choreography by Mazilier. First performed at the Paris Opéra, 1837.

The Second Empire ballet coincided with the reign of the third Napoleon and was the last gasp of the French school before it was swept away by the coming Russian school. The Paris Opéra was declining in quality because dancers such as Zina Richard, wife of the dancer and choreographer Louis Merante, and Louise Marquet (see entry 71) were never able to achieve the excellence of the ballerinas of the Romantic era. It is interesting that the Russian Zina Richard was one of the few ballerinas to emigrate from Russia to Paris and stay there for the remainder of her life.

71a. Marie-Alexandre Alophe
1812 - 1883
Colored lithograph
$11^{1}/_{8}$ x $8^{3}/_{8}$

Louise Marquet in *Marco Spada* (see entry 70).

b. Disdéri
Photographs (2)
$4^{1}/_{8}$ x $2^{3}/_{8}$

Louise Marquet in unidentified costumes.

Louise Marquet (b. 1857) danced innumerable roles in her eighteen-year career at the Paris Opéra but remains a minor figure in the history of dance. The photographs of Marquet in costume are typical of the early use of photography for commercial purposes.

72. Unknown Artist
c. 1880
Color lithograph from photograph
$11^{5}/_{8}$ x $9^{1}/_{4}$

Costume sketch of Charles Müller as Carlo in *Santanella*.

The costume worn by Charles Müller in this ballet derived from costumes of the Baroque period when the male dancer first appeared in tights. The Russian ballet dancer still wears a similar costume.

73. Unknown Artist
Watercolor
$10^{1}/_{8}$ x $7^{1}/_{2}$

Costume sketch of Zina Richard for an unidentified ballet.

The female costume underwent a major change when Taglioni appeared in *La Sylphide* (see entry 53). The long gauze skirt became the conventional female costume until the reforms of Diaghilev. In the nineteenth century, a greater concern with historical accuracy resulted from the archaeological research of Charles Kean in England and Paul Lorimer, designer at the Paris Opéra, in France. The elaborate costume was still in vogue for certain ballets as is apparent in this costume sketch of Zina Richard.

53

74. Alfred Grévin
1827 - 1892
Pencil sketch
8⁷/₈ x 5¹/₄

A Dancer in a Butterfly Costume.

Alfred Grévin was a designer of costumes and a cartoonist who enjoyed great success with his designs. They were reproduced often in contemporary newspapers and magazines.

54

75a

75a. C. Wilhelm
1859 - 1925
Watercolor
8¹/₂ x 5¹/₂

Faust. Costume sketch for Mephistopheles. First performed at the Empire Theatre, London, 1895.

b. Watercolor
8¹/₂ x 5¹/₂

Faust. Costume sketch for one of twelve children drummers. First performed at the Empire Theatre, London, 1895.

c. Watercolor
8¹/₂ x 5¹/₂

Cinderella. Performed at the Garrick Theatre, London, 1898. Costume sketch for Ghisbe.

d. Watercolor
8¹/₂ x 5¹/₂

Round the Town Again. Performed at the Empire Theatre, London, 1899. Costume sketch for "Spring Onion," Salad Set.

e. Watercolor
8¹/₂ x 5¹/₂

Spring Chicken. Performed at the Empire Theatre, London, 1905. Costume sketch for Miss Holly, Marveilleuse Model.

f. Watercolor
8⁷/₈ x 6

Belle of the Ball. Performed at the Empire Theatre, London, 1907. Costume sketch for a Parasol Lady.

The Empire Theatre was the center for Victorian ballet. William John Charles Pitcher, known as C. Wilhelm, played an important role at the Empire from 1887 to 1915 as librettist and designer of costumes and settings. His costume designs were imaginative adaptations of historical costumes, descriptive representations of material objects, and detailed conceptions executed in soft and delicate tonalities. Many of Wilhelm's sketches have survived and thus are able to serve as a documentation of the period's social aesthetic.

75b

75d

76a. Julius Hansen
active first quarter 20th century
Watercolor
$13^{1}/_{2}$ x 10

Bacchus by Jules Massenet. Choreography by
Massenet. Sketch of four dances.

b. Watercolor
$13^{5}/_{8}$ x $9^{3}/_{8}$

Bacchus. Sketch for twenty-four Bacchantes, Final
March, first tableau.

In comparison to most of the costume sketches in the
exhibition which isolate the costume design for a
single figure, these are working sketches conceived as
a unity within the performance. The drawing of the
twenty-four figures shows the repetition of the
costume as it would appear on the stage.

77. Unknown Artist
Colored engraving
$9^{1}/_{2}$ x $12^{1}/_{2}$

Toy theatre sheet for *Jack and the Beanstalk*.

Toy theatre sheets reproduced in detailed miniature
the costumes and scenery of nineteenth century stage
productions. Each set was composed of ten to twenty
sheets mounted on cardboard which would then be cut
out so that the performance could be re-enacted in a toy
theatre version. At its height, fifty publishers produced
toy theatre sheets; however, as they increased in
popularity, the quality of the work declined. By the
second half of the nineteenth century, they were
included in magazines or inexpensively printed on a
single sheet. Early hand-colored examples have
retained the bright tones that vividly record the history
of nineteenth century theatre.

Ballet in America

The Puritan tradition held fast in young America, but history shows that the natural propensity for rhythmic expression through dance can never be long suppressed.

Our independence declared, we began to receive regular shipments of dancers and teachers with no mean assist from the French Revolution which scattered French culture far and wide.

By the 1820s, we were hosting the Petipa family, the Taglioni family (Paul and his wife), and later the Cecchetti family with the infant Enrico in tow. The latter actually got up and down the Mississippi as far north as St. Paul.

When the European sensation Fanny Elssler came in 1840, she received a tumultuous reception and stayed for two years, amassing the bulk of her personal fortune and visiting every major southern and northern city of the day.

Less than two decades later, we played host to a stranded ballet company in New York (not a hack group at that!) and fashioned *The Black Crook* for them, the greatest musical sensation of the century and the immediate forerunner of the American musical comedy.

It ran for fifty years by which time we had nurtured and produced our own great pioneers, Isadora Duncan, Loie Fuller, Ruth St. Denis.

83

78. Program for *The Black Crook.*

The Black Crook by C. M. Barras. Choreography by David Costa. First performed by Marie Bonfanti and Rita Sangalli at Niblo's Garden, New York, 1866.

It is possible that *The Black Crook* was the first American musical comedy. The scenery was originally created for the production *La Biche au Bois;* and was purchased by William Wheatley after that production was cancelled. Wheatley created *The Black Crook,* a melodrama based on a Faustian theme. The extravaganza achieved immediate popularity because of the elaborate staging, ran for 475 performances in New York, and toured almost continually until 1909. Its influence could be seen everywhere, as in the advertisement (see entry no. 83) for Black Crook cigars.

79. Unknown Artist
Lithograph
8 x 6⁶/₈

Portrait of Rita Sangalli.

See entry 78.

80. Unknown Artist
Color lithograph
13¹/₄ x 10³/₈

Music cover for "Black Crook Lancers."

See entry 78.

81. Unknown Artist
Color lithograph
13¹/₄ x 10¹/₈

Music cover for "Black Crook Waltzes."

See entry 78.

82. Unknown Artist
Wood engraving
7¹/₈ x 11¹/₈

Newspaper illustration of Niblo's Gardens, New York.

See entry 78.

83. Advertisement for Black Crook cigars.
Lithograph
6³/₄ x 4¹/₄

See entry 78.

60

85

84a. Abraham Walkowitz
      1880 - 1965
      Watercolor
      $8^3/_8$ x 4

      Isadora Duncan.

  b. Watercolor
      $8^1/_2$ x 4

      Isadora Duncan.

      Isadora Duncan (1878 - 1927) developed a unique individual style of dance that revolted against conventional restrictions associated with classical ballet. Each movement in her dances was prompted by emotions and nature and therefore, each dance could never be exactly repeated. An American by birth, she spent a major part of her life abroad and was enthusiastically received by her admirers in Paris, Budapest, Berlin, St. Petersburg, Moscow, and other European cities. Although Isadora Duncan left no school or distinguished pupils, she prepared the path and served as inspiration for future modern dancers.

85.   José Clara
      1878 - 1958
      Pen and ink
      $10^5/_8$ x $8^1/_8$

      Isadora Duncan.

      Isadora Duncan was an inspiration to sculptors, painters, and writers, as well as dancers. Many artists recorded her on paper and in print. In this work, one of several executed for a book of drawings of the dancer, Duncan is pictured in her classic Greek-inspired costume. She usually danced in a simple, flowing tunic and barefoot, an innovation she introduced to the Western stage.

86.   Paul Burlin
      1886 - 1969
      Ink sketch heightened in white
      $9^7/_8$ x $12^6/_8$

      Décor for an unidentified production.

      This décor by Paul Burlin differs from scenic designs of the past in its freedom of expression. Burlin, one of the first artists to be interested in the art of the American Southwest, lived in Paris from 1921 to 1932 and shared a studio with the Cubist painter Albert Gleizes. Later, his work became more expressionistic. As is evident in this sketch, twentieth century scenic design, like that of the preceding four centuries, continued to be influenced by and a reflection of contemporary art forms.

87.   Jared Lee
      Watercolor
      13 x $17^5/_8$

      Scenes Seen (A Bicentennial Ballet) by George Verdak. Choreography by Verdak. Décor by Jared Lee. Music by Vittorio Rieti. Performed at Clowes Hall, Butler University, Indianapolis, 1976.

      In honor of the United State's two-hundredth birthday, George Verdak, Director of the Indianapolis Ballet Theater, created Scenes Seen (A Bicentennial Ballet). The decor and costumes attest to the artistic freedom allowed the stage designer of the 1970s.

88.   Eugene Berman
      1899 - 1973
      Ink drawing
      $10^7/_8$ x $8^3/_8$

      Figure drawing made for George Verdak for a poster or brochure cover, c. 1949.

      The Russian-American painter Eugene Berman was closely associated with American theatre. He designed sets and costumes for George Balanchine ballets performed by the American Ballet and for the New York Metropolitan Opera. In addition, he designed the interior for the theatre at the Ringling Museum in Sarasota, Florida. This particular drawing was executed for a poster or brochure cover.

Theatrical and Social Dance

If Europe was not too enterprising in the matter of exporting serious dancers after the visit of Elssler, we kept the ball rolling neatly with a never ending succession of popular social dance forms—variations on the waltz and polka were never ending.

If the ballet declined in France, theatrical dance was able to fill the void as in the case of the hysterical success of the cancan. The developer of the form was Betty Rigolboche who spawned dozens of successors, the delight of the fascinated Lautrec.

89

89. Henri de Toulouse-Lautrec
1864 - 1901
Lithograph
15³/₄ x 11³/₄

Mlle. Lender Dancing the Bolero.

In the latter part of the nineteenth century, the bourgeosie frequented music halls to see performances of the cancan and other popular dances. Toulouse-Lautrec often appeared at the Moulin Rouge where he sought to capture its spirit in drawings, paintings, posters, and lithographs. Some of the dancers he sketched over and over again were Loie Fuller, La Goulue, Marcelle Lender, and Jane Avril. Simultaneously recording the classic ballet was his fellow Impressionist artist Edgar Degas.

90a. Frédéric Sorrieu
b. 1807
after Anaïs Colin
1822 - 1899
Color lithograph
10³/₈ x 8¹/₈

La Polka.

b. Color lithograph
10¹/₄ x 8¹/₈

La Polka.

Although the ancestry of the nineteenth century popular version of the polka can be traced back to seventeenth century Scandinavia, its immediate predecessors could be found in the country dances of Czechoslovakia and Poland. From Prague, it was taken to Paris in 1840 where it was transformed by dancing masters such as Cellarius (see entry 67). Cellarius brought it to London and soon the polka craze swept both Western Europe and America.

91. Sapphir (?)
Pencil drawing
8³/₄ x 11¹/₈

"Allow me the pleasure of dancing the next polka with you?", 1844.

See entry 90.

90b

92. Richard Doyle
    1824 - 1883
    Pencil drawing
    8¹/₈ x 10⁷/₈

    Polka.

    See entry 90.

93a. Charles Vernier
     1831 - 1887
     Color lithograph
     13¹/₈ x 10

     Cartoon of "La Rigolbochomanie" and the CanCan.

  b. Color lithograph
     13¹/₈ x 10

     Cartoon of "La Rigolbochomanie" and the CanCan.

     Betty Rigolboche, the originator of the nineteenth century French cancan, became the center of a Parisian craze called "La Rigolbochomanie." In the nineteenth century as in the preceding centuries (see entries 48-51), popular dancers and dances were often the subject of the caricaturist's pen.

92

Diaghilev's Ballets Russes

Sensing that Russian ballet, like the French before it, might succumb to its own tradition-bound inertia, the brilliant Diaghilev grasped the reins of change earlier on than Noverre and the other reformers did.

Diaghilev rooted out Russia's finest artists in all categories and transported them to Paris, where free from all formal restraint, he let choreographer, composer, and designer have free rein, though he always kept a watchful eye over their productions.

The result was the fantastic series of Russian triumphs which focused world attention on such luminaries as Nijinsky, Stravinsky, Bakst, Fokine, Benois, and later included rising European artists Picasso, Braque, and a host of others.

The fetters were off, Diaghilev left us an untrammeled blank canvas on which the thoughts of the twentieth century could be expressed.

The artist who executed the work included in the exhibition is given in the first part of the entry. The designer(s) of the original décor and costumes after which they are drawn are noted in the second part of the entry.

94. Michel Larionov
1881 - 1964
Pencil drawing
$10^1/_8$ x 8

Portrait of Diaghilev.

The early career of Serge Diaghilev (1872 - 1929) witnessed the founding of an art magazine *Mir Isskustva (The World of Art)* with Léon Bakst, Alexandre Benois and others, the editing of the *Imperial Theatres' Yearbook,* the organization of art exhibitions, and his first experiences as an impresario of the theatre. In 1909, the Ballet Russe de Serge de Diaghilev was formed. The company, under Diaghilev's direction, coordinated the efforts of outstanding artists from all fields into a unified whole. The Ballets Russes introduced the art of Russian ballet to Western Europe and Paris, the company's home, was transformed again into "the world capital of dance." The Ballets Russes disbanded after the death of Diaghilev in 1929.

95. Unknown Artist
Etching
$9^7/_8$ x $7^3/_4$

Portrait of Michel Fokine.

In the eighteenth century, Noverre unified the elements of ballet, dancing, pantomime, and music; in the twentieth century, the Russian dancer and choreographer Michel Fokine (1880 - 1442) also sought for a unification, "a unity of expression, a unity which is made up of harmonious blending of the three elements — music, painting, and plastic art." His ideas were rejected by the Imperial Theatre management, but advocated by Diaghilev. Fokine choreographed for the Ballets Russes for the first time in 1909, a year which marked the beginning of a new era in ballet predicated on the choreographer's principles of reform.

96a. Dorothy Mullock
Woodcut
$8^1/_4$ x $5^1/_8$

Le Spectre de la Rose by Jean Louis Vaudoyer adapted from a poem by Théophile Gautier. Choreography by Michel Fokine. Décor and costumes by Léon Bakst. First performed by Vaslav Nijinsky and Tamara Karsavina at the Théâtre de Monte Carlo, 1911. Costume design for Nijinsky.

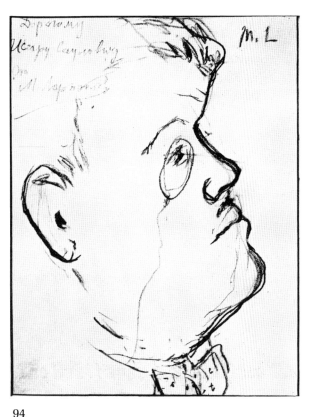

94

b. Woodcut
8¼ x 5¼

Après-midi d'un Faune by Vaslav Nijinsky. Choreography by Nijinsky. Décor by Léon Bakst. First performed by Ballets Russes with Nijinsky at Théâtre du Châtelet, Paris, 1912. Costume design for Nijinsky.

The fame of Vaslav Nijinsky (1890 - 1950) rests on his phenomenally successful nine-year career with the Ballets Russes. The development of a mental disease in 1916 from which he never recovered brought his career to an abrupt end. Nijinsky, as choreographer and dancer, possessed exceptional talents. He was noted for his elevation, *ballon,* the ability to rebound into the air after a jump, and remarkable pirouettes. His interpretive ability and talent to become the character which he was dancing, made him the perfect dancer to fulfill Fokine's ideas. Nijinsky, during his short career, was responsible for reviving the status of the male dancer.

97. Vaslav Nijinsky
1890 - 1950
Crayon sketch
14¾ x 11¼

This drawing was executed by Nijinsky during his years at a sanitorium.

98. Ernst Oppler
1867 - 1929
Etching
8½ x 7

Tamara Karsavina dancing a Polka.

The magnificence of the Ballets Russes was due in part to the brilliant partnership of Tamara Karsavina (b. 1885) and Nijinsky. Both were excellent interpretive artists capable of performing classic ballet, the modern works of Fokine, and those ballets choreographed to the music of such moderns as Igor Stravinsky and Rimsky-Korsakov. Karsavina's career began with lessons at the Russian Imperial schools and continued as a dancer at the Maryinsky Theatre, but it was as a principal ballerina for the Ballets Russes that she achieved lasting fame. In 1931, she retired permanently.

99. Ludwig Kainer
active 20th century
Color lithograph
18 x 12¼

Cléopâtre by Michel Fokine. Choreography by Fokine. Décor and costumes by Léon Bakst. First performed at Maryinsky Theatre, St. Petersburg, 1908, under the title *Une Nuit d'Egypt.* Décor from *Russichen Ballet Portfolio.*

The décor and costumes for Cléopâtre were the first created by Léon Bakst (1866 - 1924) for the Ballets Russes. He was a close friend of Diaghilev's and co-founder of *Mir Isskustva,* the magazine which first expressed the ideas of Diaghilev and his concept of total theatre. The concurrence of the two artists enabled Bakst to execute designs which complemented and enhanced the choreography, music, and movement of the ballet. Some of his greatest designs were for *Carnaval* (see entry 105c), *Le Spectre de la Rose* (see entry 96a), *Schéhérazade* (see entry 105a), and *Après Midi d'un Faune.* (see entry 96b).

100. Ludwig Kainer
active 20th century
Color lithograph
16 x 11¾

Petrouchka by Igor Stravinsky and Alexandre Benois. Choreography by Michel Fokine. Décor and costumes by Benois. First performed by Ballets Russes with Vaslav Nijinsky, Tamara Karsavina, and Enrico Cecchetti at the Théâtre du Châtelet, Paris, 1911. Décor from *Russichen Ballet Portfolio.*

Alexandre Benois (1870 - 1960), the third founding member of *Mir Isskustva,* began his career as a scenic designer for the Maryinsky Theatre. As members of the Ballets Russes, Benois and Bakst created a new standard of stage design. According to the contemporary English ballet critic Richard Buckle: "Benois stands for romantic evolution, for the influence of the French eighteenth century on Peter's capital, and for the Russian *fin de siècle* which was also a *renaissance.*" This *renaissance* was carried to Paris and other cities of Western Europe and the United States by the Ballets Russes where it created a distinctive chapter in twentieth century ballet history.

69

101. Eileen Mayo
Tempera drawing
13¹/₂ x 14³/₄

La Chatte by Sobeka (Henri Sanguet, Boris Kochno,
George Balanchine) after an Aesop Fable.
Choreography by George Balanchine. Décor and
costumes by Naum Gabo and Antoine Pevsner. First
performed by Ballets Russes with Serge Lifar and Olga
Spessivtzeva at Théâtre de Monte Carlo, 1927. Design
for a décor.

Constructivism, originally a Russian art movement that
was based on the premise that movement in space
represented by pure geometric forms was more
important than volume, was adapted to stage design by
artists such as Naum Gabo (b. 1890) and Antoine
Pevsner (1886 - 1962). The Constructivist setting was
characterized by its functionalism, simplicity, and
elimination of almost all detail. The basic utilitarian
structural form usually remained on stage throughout
the performance.

102. André Derain
      1880 - 1954
      Silk screen
      20½ x 24⅞

La Concurrence by André Derain. Choreography by
George Balanchine. Décor and costumes by Derain.
First performed by René Blum and Colonel de Basil
Ballet Russe at Théâtre de Monte Carlo, 1932. Design
for an act curtain.

After the death of Diaghilev in 1929, the company of
Diaghilev's Ballets Russes disbanded. In the same
year, but after Diaghilev's death, René Blum
(1884 - 1944) was appointed director of the Ballets de
l'Opéra de Monte Carlo. In 1931, he accepted Colonel
W. de Basil as a partner. George Balanchine and
Leonide Massine choreographed for the new company
of Russian dancers. In 1936, René Blum disassociated
himself from the company. For the next twenty-six
years, the Ballet Russe continued with numerous
changes in directors, choreographers, and dancers.
The last performances of the Ballet Russe were during
the 1962 - 1963 season.

103. Mariano Andreu
      b. 1901
      Tempera
      10⅝ x 14½

Don Juan by Eric Allatini and Michel Fokine. Based
on the play by Molière. Choreography by Michel
Fokine. Décor and costumes by Mariano Andreu. First
performed by René Blum's Ballet Russe at Alhambra
Theatre, London, 1936. Design for a décor.

Unlike many of the Ballet Russe productions, *Don
Juan* was based on a classic eighteenth century play by
Molière with music by Christoph Wilbald Gluck
(1761). Eric Allatini, after an intensive search
throughout Europe, located Gluck's complete score
which was composed to follow the Molière play. It was
then revised by Allatini and Fokine.

104. T.H. Capiero
      Watercolor
      12¾ x 7¾

Cléopâtre (see entry 99). Performed by Vaslav
Nijinsky, Anna Pavlova, Ida Rubinstein, and Michel
Fokine at Théâtre du Châtelet, Paris, 1909. Costume
design of Nijinsky.

See entry 96.

105a. Ethelbert White
active 20th century
Watercolor
10⁵/₈ x 7³/₈

Cléopâtre (see entry 99). Latin American Tour with Lubov Tchernicheva and Leonide Massine, 1917 - 1918. Costume sketch of Tchernicheva.

b. Watercolor
10³/₄ x 7

Schéhérazade by Alexandre Benois. Choreography by Michel Fokine. Décor and costumes by Léon Bakst. First performed by Ballets Russes with Ida Rubinstein and Vaslav Nijinsky at the Paris Opéra, 1910. Costume sketch of Lubov Tchernicheva.

c. Watercolor
13³/₄ x 9³/₄

Le Carnaval by Michel Fokine. Choreography by Michel Fokine. Décor and costumes by Léon Bakst. Performed by Ballets Russes with Vaslav Nijinsky, Adolph Bolm, and Tamara Karsavina at Paris Opéra, 1910. Costume sketch of Adolph Bolm.

Lubov Tchernicheva (b. 1890) and Adolph Bolm (1884 - 1951) were principal dancers with Diaghilev's Ballets Russes. Both Tchernicheva and Bolm are depicted here (Schérérazade) in roles for which they are most famous.

106a. Nathalie Gontcharova
1881 - 1962
Charcoal drawing
30¹/₄ x 15¹/₄

Le Coq d'Or by V. Bielsky, revised by Alexandre Benois. Based on a poem by Pushkin. Décor by Nathalie Gontcharova. First performed by Ballets Russes with Tamara Karsavina and Enrico Cecchetti at the Paris Opéra, 1914. Costume sketch of the Queen of Shemâkhan (Karsavina).

b. Charcoal sketch
30¹/₄ x 12¹/₄

Le Coq d'Or. Costume sketch of the Astrologer (Cecchetti).

The 1914 production of Le Coq d'Or was unique for its use of a double cast. One to act and dance and the other to serve as a vocal counterpart. Benois devised this method to prevent ''the mismatching, which too often becomes disturbing in opera, of unattractive heroes and heroines.'' Thus the characters were presented on the stage by dancers who could act and the singers were hidden in the orchestra pit. The décor and costumes designed by Gontcharova were noteworthy for their brilliant color, fantasy, and decorative quality.

107a. Randolph Schwabe
b. 1885
Watercolor
11³/₈ x 7⁷/₈

Parade by Jean Cocteau. Choreography by Leonide Massine. Décor and costumes by Pablo Picasso. First performed by Ballets Russes at Théatre du Châtelet with Lydia Lopoukhova and Massine, Paris, 1917. Costume design of Chinese magician (Massine).

b. Watercolor
14¹/₂ x 10⁷/₈

The Sleeping Princess by Nicholas Sergeyev (a revival of The Sleeping Beauty). Choreography by Petipa and Bronislava Nijinska. Décor by Léon Bakst. Performed by Ballets Russes with Lydia Lopoukhova and Stanislas Idzikowski at Alhambra Theatre, London, 1921. Costume design of Blue Bird (Idzikowski).

c Watercolor
12³/₈ x 9¹/₂

Midnight Sun by Leonide Massine. Choreography by Massine. Décor and costumes by Michel Larionov. First performed by Ballets Russes at Grand Theatre, Geneva, 1915. Costume design.

It is possible that these costume sketches of individual dancers and those executed by Ethelbert White (see entry 105) were done for the ballet publisher Beaumont. The reproductions of the drawings were meant to be mounted on plywood, cut out, and set on a platform to be used as a shelf decoration.

108.   Randolph Schwabe
       b. 1885
       Pencil, ink, and watercolor
       10 x 10¹/₂

Parade (see entry 107a). Costume design.

Diaghilev's designers of décors and costumes turned
away from the classic ballet to introduce new ideas in
these theatrical arts. Ballets Russes collaborators were
often the foremost contemporary Russian and
European artists such as Pablo Picasso, Michel
Larionov (see entries 107e and 112) and his wife
Nathalie Gontcharova (see entry 106), André Derain
(see entry 102), Marie Laurencin (see entry 130),
Naum Gabo and Antoine Pevsner (see entries 101 and
109), and Georges Braque. The designs of Benois (see
entries 100 and 105) and Bakst (see entries 99, 107b,
and 111), permanent members of Diaghilev's
company, often reflected exotic, foreign influences.

109. Eileen Mayo
      Gouache
      7⅝ x 12½

      La Chatte (see entry 101). Costume design.

      This costume design by Gabo and Pevsner, like the architectural constuctions for the ballet (see entry 101), was an expression of Constructivist philosophy. Their designs and the performance was described by one critic as "a geometric problem . . . a mathematical pattern," by another as "an exercise in pure plastique, deliberately devoid of story, which reduces scenery and costume to so artful a minimum that you scarcely notice the absence of either."

110. Alexander Ekster
      Pencil drawing
      18⅛ x 14½

      Don Juan, Cubist version by the Moscow Art Theatre. Costume design.

      See entry 103.

111. Léon Bakst
      1866 - 1924
      Pencil and gouache
      9¾ x 6¾

      La Péri by Théophile Gautier and Jean Coralli. Choreography by Fokine. Performed by Ballets Russes, Paris, 1911. Costume sketch of Nijinsky.

      See entry 99.

112. Michel Larionov
      1881 - 1964
      Silk screen
      19¾ x 12¾

      Stencil sketch for an animal costume in Diaghilev's unrealized ballet *Les Histoires Naturelles.*

      Russian born Michel Larionov moved to Paris in 1914 when he became closely associated with the Ballets Russes. In addition to this unrealized ballet, Larionov did designs for *The Midnight Sun* (see entry 107c), *Contes Russes, Le Renard,* and others.

111

113. Nicolas Remisov
Watercolor
12$^7/_8$ x 8$^7/_8$

One of three costume designs for a Russian peasant.

The two designs by Remisov (entries 113 and 114) are representative of two parallel trends in the Ballets Russes, the interest in folklore and the interest in contemporary art movements.

114. Nicolas Remisov
Pencil
14$^1/_2$ x 11$^1/_2$

Design for Cubist costume. Solo dance.

See entry 113.

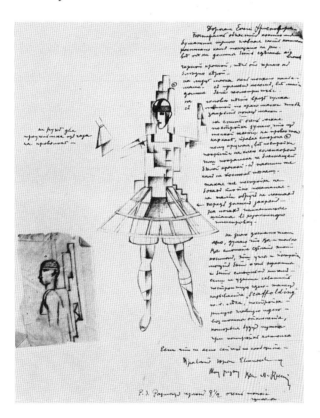

114

115. Ernst Oppler
1867 - 1929
Etching
6$^1/_8$ x 9$^1/_4$

Giselle (see entry 64). Décor and costumes by Alexandre Benois. Performed by Ballets Russes with Tamara Karsavina and Vaslav Nijinsky at the Royal Opéra, Covent Garden, London, 1911.

The Ballets Russes' London production of the Romantic ballet *Giselle* was generally criticized except for the performance of Karsavina and Nijinsky. The ballet itself was considered old-fashioned; the audience preferred the "art nouveau" ballet, not the French Romantic tradition.

116. Troy Kinney
1871 - 1938
Etching
9$^1/_2$ x 11$^1/_4$

Le Spectre de la Rose (see entry 96a). Performed by Fokine and Fokina, c. 1920.

Troy Kinney, American artist and writer on dance, is known for his many etchings and dry-points on subjects relating to the dance. He is equally respected for his writings and lectures in the same field.

117. Willy Pogany
1882 - 1955
Letterpress
22 x 14

Poster for Diaghilev's Ballets Russes, American Tour by arrangement with the Metropolitan Opera Company.

The first American tour of Diaghilev's Ballets Russes occurred in 1916, but without the two dancers America wanted to see most — Nijinsky and Karsavina. The tour took them to New York, Boston, Albany, Detroit, Chicago, Cincinnati, Washington, D.C., Philadelphia, and six other cities. On its return tour, Nijinsky joined the company. The success of the American tours of Diaghilev's Ballets Russes increased the public's awareness of the brilliance of this art form.

118. Hoppe
      Autographed photograph
      $7^{7}/_{8}$ x $5^{7}/_{8}$

      Portrait of Anna Pavlova

      Anna Pavlova (1881 - 1931) studied at the Russian
      Imperial School of Ballet, became a prima ballerina in
      1906 after a performance of *Swan Lake,* and in 1907,
      began her first appearances outside of Russia. She
      danced for one season with the Ballets Russes (1909),
      established a permanent residence in London in 1912,
      and in 1913, danced for the last time in Russia at the
      Maryinsky Theatre. Pavlova danced in cities
      throughout the world and whenever she danced she
      was acclaimed. Basically conservative and classic in
      her approach to ballet, she was noted for an individual
      style that was graceful and sincere. Each performance
      appeared effortless and spontaneous, despite the
      numerous times it might have been danced. Pavlova,
      more than any other single artist, was responsible for
      inspiring generations of dancers and expanding the
      ballet audience.

119. Ernst Oppler
      1867 - 1929
      Drypoint
      $19^{1}/_{8}$ x $15^{1}/_{4}$

      The Dying Swan by Michel Fokine. An extract from
      the music of Camille Saint-Saëns' *Le Carnaval des
      Animaux.* Costume by Léon Bakst. First performed by
      Anna Pavlova at a special performance in the Hall of
      Noblemen, St. Petersburg, 1905.

      The Dying Swan, a solo dance created by Fokine for
      Pavlova, is synonymous with the dancer's name. When
      first choreographed, the work was "revolutionary"
      because, as Fokine stated in 1934, it "illustrated
      admirably the transition between the old and the new,
      for here I make use of the technique of the old dance
      and the traditional costume, and a highly developed
      technique is necessary, but the purpose of the dance is
      not to display that technique but to create the symbol of
      the everlasting struggle in this life and all that is
      mortal . . . it appeals not merely to the eye but to the
      emotions and imagination." Anna Pavlova in *The
      Dying Swan* became a new symbol of post-Romantic
      ballet.

Décors and Books

80

Cap. Esgangarato. Cap.^o Cocodrillo.²

123

120. Eugene Berman
1899 - 1973

Devil's Holiday by Vincenzo Tommasini. Choreography by Frederick Ashton. Décor and costumes by Eugene Berman. First performed by the Ballet Russe de Monte Carlo, Metropolitan Opera House, 1939. Décor.

When the designer and the choreographer agree on final sketches for ballet scenery, the drawings are sent to a scenic artist, a highly skilled technical painter who is often a designer himself. After reaching a predetermined degree of completion, the designer would do the last few strokes himself and, as in the case of the Dali décor, occasionally sign the completed work.

121. Salvador Dali
b. 1904

Bacchanale by Salvador Dali. Choreography by Leonide Massine. Décor by Dali. First performed by the Ballet Russe de Monte Carlo, Metropolitan Opera House, 1939. Décor.

See entry 120.

122. Fabrito Caroso
Nobiltà di Dame
1605

A book of dances with text and music written and published for the Duke and Duchess of Parma and Piacenza, 1605.

123. Jacques Callot
Balli di Sfessania
c. 1622

An original copy of a series of twenty-four etchings relating to the Italian *commedia dell'arte*.

124. *Proserpine*
1680

A commemorative volume with engravings for a production presented before the King at Saint Germain en Laye. Printed by Christophe Ballard, sole printer of music for the King.

125. Pierre Rameau
Le Maître à Danser
1734

A guide to social dancing containing principles of dance with engravings of various postures including the five basic positions.

126. M. Magny
Principes de Chorégraphie
1765

An original manuscript with dance notations for choreographic principles.

127. Carlo Blasis
Notes Upon Dancing
(translation from the original French and Italian by R. Barton)
1847

An historical and practical treatise on Ballet with a history of the Imperial and Royal Academy of Dancing at Milan, biographical notes on the Blasis Family, and passages on theatrical art.

128a. Ballet Program for a season of Russian ballet. Royal Opera, Covent Garden, London.
July 7, 1911

b. *Comedia Illustré*
Special issue dedicated to the Ballets Russes
May 20, 1914

c. Official Program
Benefit Performance for the Red Cross, Great Britain by the Ballet Russe
Théâtre National de L'Opéra
December 29, 1915

d. Ballet Program
Benefit Performance by the Ballets Russes
Théâtre du Châtelet
May, 1917

e. Official Program for the Season
Théâtre de Monte Carlo
1924

129. Arabella Yorke
The Art of Lydia Lopokova
1920

A souvenir volume including a portrait by Pablo Picasso, an essay by Cyril W. Beaumont, and costume sketches.

130. Marie Laurencin
Les Biches
1924

A two volume edition for *Les Biches*, performed by Diaghilev's Ballets Russes with curtain, décor, and costumes by Marie Laurencin.

131. George Barbier
Vingt-Cinq Costumes pour Le Théâtre
1927

A limited edition of colored costume sketches for seven different productions.

Deuxieme tems des bras du Menu

125

Bibliography

Blanchard, Jeffrey. "Theater Section," *Jacques Callot: Prints & Related Drawings.* Washington, D.C.: National Gallery of Art, 1975.

Balanchine, George. *Balanchine's New Complete Stories of the Great Ballets.* Edited by Francis Mason. New York: Doubleday Company, Inc., 1968.

Beaumont, Cyril W. *Complete Book of Ballets, A Guide to the Principal Ballets of the Nineteenth and Twentieth Centuries.* New York: G.P. Putnam's Sons, 1938.

Benezit, E. *Dictionnaire Critique et Documentaire des Peintres, Sculpteurs, Dessinateurs et Graveurs,* revised edition. France: Librarie Grund, 1949.

Cheney, Sheldon. *The Theatre, Three Thousand Years of Drama, Acting and Stagecraft.* New York: Tudor Publishing Company, 1929.

Chujoy, Anatole and P. W. Manchester, eds. *The Dance Encyclopedia,* revised and enlarged edition. New York: Simon and Schuster, 1967.

Freedley, George and John A. Reeves. *A History of the Theatre.* New York: Crown Publishers, 1941.

Hartnoll, Phyllis, ed. *The Oxford Companion to the Theatre.* London: Oxford University Press, 1951.

Kochno, Boris. *Diaghilev and the Ballets Russes.* Harper & Row, Publishers, Inc., 1970.

Macdonald, Nesta. *Diaghilev Observed by Critics in England and the United States 1911 - 1929.* New York: Dance Horizons, 1975.

Migel, Parmenia. *The Ballerinas, From the Court of Louis XIV to Pavlova.* New York: The Macmillan Company, 1972.

Moore, Lillian. *Artists of the Dance.* New York: Thomas Y. Crowell Company, 1938.

Murray, Peter and Linda. *A Dictionary of Art and Artists.* Harmondsworth, England: Penguin Books Ltd., 1971.

Raffe, W. G. and M. E. Purdon. *Dictionary of the Dance.* New York: A. S. Barnes and Company, 1964.

Sorell, Walter. *The Dance Through the Ages.* New York: Grosset & Dunlap, Inc., 1967.

Terry, Walter. *Ballet, A New Guide to the Liveliest Art.* New York: Dell Publishing Co., Inc., 1959.

Index